Really Useful English Words

David Maule

Penguin Quick Guides Series Editors:
Andy Hopkins and Jocelyn Potter

PENGUIN ENGLISH

Pearson Education Limited
Edinburgh Gate
Harlow
Essex CM20 2JE, England
and Associated Companies throughout the world.

ISBN 0 582 46891 4

First published 2001
3 5 7 9 10 8 6 4 2
Text copyright © David Maule 2001

The moral right of the author has been asserted.

Produced for the publisher by Bluestone Press, Charlbury, UK.
Designed and typeset by White Horse Graphics, Charlbury, UK.
Illustrations by Roger Fereday (Linda Rogers Associates).
Photography by Patrick Ellis.
Printed and bound in China NPCC/02

Published by Pearson Education Limited in association with
Penguin Books Ltd, both companies being subsidiaries of Pearson plc.

For a complete list of the titles available from Penguin English visit
our website at www.penguinenglish.com, or please write to your local
Pearson Education office or to: Marketing Department, Penguin Longman
Publishing, 80 Strand London, WC2R 0RL.

Contents

Quality high-quality • old-fashioned • reliable • stylish
well-made
Bargain store closing-down sale • discount • pricey • reduce
special offer
How to pay bank card • cash • cheque • credit card • loan
Complaining complain • credit note • exchange • faulty
receipt • refund

4 Travel and transport

The airport baggage hall • boarding pass • check-in desk
customs • departure lounge • passport control
Railway station change • direct • first-class • return • single
standard
Holiday hotel air conditioning • double room
en suite • minibar • single room • suite
Fun in the sun barbecue • cruise • excursion • picnic
sightseeing • sunbathing
Getting home bomb scare • delay • divert • strand • strike

5 Friends and family

Names first name • maiden name • middle name
nickname • surname
Relations brother-in-law • half-sister • step-brother
step-mother • step-sister
Mates classmate • colleague • flatmate • room-mate • workmate
Relationships boyfriend • ex-husband • fiancé/fiancée
partner • wife-to-be
Feelings can't stand • fall out with • fancy • make up

Visibility bright • dull • foggy • overcast • sunny
Snow and stuff blizzard • hail • sleet • slush • snowdrift

A new job accept • apply • offer • promote • turn down
Making a living deal with • do for a living • in charge of
make a living • run
Company man company director • manager • skilled
unskilled • white-collar
Nine to five flexi-time • full-time • job share • nine-to-five
part-time • shifts
All gone away early retirement • make redundant
maternity leave • resign • sack • sick leave

On TV cable • commercial • public • satellite • terrestrial
On the phone call back • hold the line • leave a message
put through • try a number
Sunday papers editorial • feature • magazine • quality
sports section • tabloid
Films dub • set • shoot • show • subtitle
Technology cybercafe • digital camera • download
e-mail address • online

Getting started

How can this book help you?

Do you want to learn more English words?
Can you say some of what you want to say …
but not all of it, because you don't know
enough words? Do you wonder where you can
find the words you need? *The Penguin Quick
Guide to Really Useful English Words* gives you
the words that you're looking for.

What's in this book?

There are over 250 really useful English words.
Each chapter looks at a different area of real
life – for example, food, clothes or travel. At
the end of every chapter you'll find exercises
to help you remember what you've learned.
And you can check your answers at the back

of the book. The key words in the book are also listed in the **Index**.

Why is this book called a *Quick Guide*?

Because it takes you straight to the words you need. For instance, we all like to eat, so why not turn to the first chapter, *Food*, starting on page 11? But don't expect to find the names of different types of food. You probably know most of these already. Instead, there are words that help you to talk about food – when you buy it in a shop or a restaurant, when you cook it and when you eat it.

This is a *Quick Guide*. You don't need to spend hours studying it. Just open it for ten minutes every day – and see how quickly you learn.

- Choose a subject that interests you. Maybe you're sitting on a bus, a train or a plane. Look at *Travel and transport*, starting on page 47. Read the chapter and find words that go with what you're doing.

- Answer the questions in the **Review** section at the end. Then go to the **Answers** section at the back of the book. Were you right?

- Now go to the **Index**. Read the sample sentences – and write down the words in your own language.

I hope you enjoy using the book. Good luck!

Food

1

In the restaurant

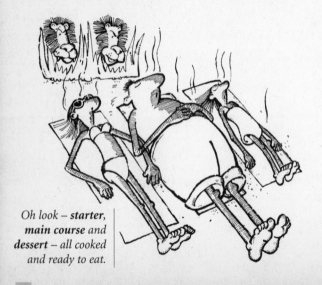

*Oh look – **starter, main course** and **dessert** – all cooked and ready to eat.*

WAITER: Would you like to see the **dinner** menu, sir?

MAN: Thank you. Hmm … I think for a **starter** I'll have Soup of the Day.

WAITER: Yes, sir. Today the soup is –

MAN: And for the **main course**, well, I had a **snack** about an hour ago, and a heavy **lunch** before that. Is the Chef's Special quite light?

WAITER: Yes, sir. Today it's –

MAN: No, don't worry – I'll eat it anyway. And for **dessert** I'll have Fruits in Season.

dinner

starter

main course

snack

lunch

dessert

How to cook fish

Fish

fry

grill

poach

steam

bake

Many people **fry** fish in a little oil, but there are many other ways of cooking it. You can **grill** it – but remember that the grill needs to be really hot before you put the fish under it. Or you can **poach** it. Just put your fish in a pan with a little white wine and water, and heat it gently for a few minutes. And a simple method is to **steam** it – wrap it in foil and place it over some boiling vegetables. 10–15 minutes should be long enough. Or why not just brush some oil or melted butter over the fish and **bake** it in the oven?

Restaurant critic

Eating Out

This week:
The Kings Head, Cardiff Bay

The chicken soup was so **salty** that I couldn't taste anything else. The steak was **overcooked** until it was very dry, and the sauce – which was supposed to be **spicy** – was actually quite **bland**. The vegetables had been boiled until they were soft – they were really **disgusting**. And the apple pie which I had for dessert was **sour** – this chef has never heard of sugar. Apart from all that, it was a nice meal. The restaurant was charming, the staff were very helpful and the coffee was really delicious.

salty

overcooked

spicy

bland

disgusting

sour

Cheese soufflé

melt

stir

simmer

grate

beat

whisk

Melt 25g of butter in a saucepan, add 25g of plain flour and stir for two minutes over a medium heat. Now slowly **stir** in 50ml of milk and let it **simmer** gently for three minutes, stirring occasionally. **Grate** 75g of hard cheese and stir this in with a little salt and pepper. Separate three eggs into yolks and whites. **Beat** the yolks and stir them in too. Now **whisk** the egg whites until they are stiff, beat a couple of spoonfuls into the sauce and carefully stir in the rest. Put the mixture in a buttered soufflé dish and bake at 190°C for 30–35 minutes.

*Well, you did say **whisk** the egg whites till they were stiff …*

Shop till you drop

MUM: Now, we need some **bars** of –

BILLY: Chocolate?

MUM: No, soap. And a few **tins** of –

BILLY: Lemonade? Coke? Fizzy orange?

MUM: Soup. Nice healthy soup.

BILLY: Can we have some **cans** too?

MUM: Very funny. They're the same thing. Now, I also want a big **packet** of –

BILLY: Chocolate biscuits?

MUM: No, washing powder, and a **tube** of toothpaste.

BILLY: Mum, you're no fun at all!

bar

tin

can

packet

tube

Review 1

A Match these words with the descriptions.

starter snack dessert lunch sour bland

1 A meal in the middle of the day.
2 Some food you eat between meals.
3 It means an acid taste – like lemon.
4 It means the food has very little taste.
5 You might begin a meal with this …
6 … and end with this.

B Match 1–5 with a–e.

1 Cook in hot oil.   a) steam
2 Cook in a hot oven.   b) fry
3 Cook in very hot water.   c) grill
4 Cook above very hot water.   d) bake
5 Cook near something   e) boil
   very hot.

Clothes

2

Witness

OFFICER: What did they look like?

WOMAN: One of them had a red and white **spotted** shirt, a **plain** jacket and **striped** trousers. Terrible!

OFFICER: And the other one?

WOMAN: He was even worse – a striped sweater – blue and pink. And **checked** trousers – can you believe it?

OFFICER: How big were the men?

WOMAN: Sorry, I only noticed their clothes. You see, I'm a fashion designer.

spotted

plain

striped

checked

The bargain hunter

Yeah, my waist's the same size as it was 20 years ago.

Look at these jeans! Only three pounds, so I got two pairs. OK, they're a bit **tight**, but I'm going to lose weight soon. No, they aren't too **short** – it's just these shoes I'm wearing. And I got this jacket for five pounds. Wait – I'll slip it on too. Yes, I admit it's quite **loose**. No, it isn't **baggy** – it's only a size bigger than normal, and I can take it in. Yes, I know it's long, but you can't have everything. And the blouse was only a pound. Tight? No – I'd say **close-fitting**. And with my figure, that's not a problem.

tight

short

loose

baggy

close-fitting

Material rap

*I wish we could change to **cotton** in the summer.*

I don't like **wool**, it isn't cool,
It makes you sweat a lot.
And **cotton**'s just impossible,
Unless your iron's hot.

I don't like **suede** in any shade
Of brown or green or grey
And get no joy from **corduroy**
Please take the stuff away!

What I like is **nylon**,
Top and trousers too,
With shirt and socks and
    underwear
In matching shades of blue.
Though people turn their heads
    and stare
I'm so relaxed that I don't care.

wool

cotton

suede

corduroy

nylon

Garden party

MR & MRS
MONTAGU-SMYTHE
HAVE PLEASURE IN INVITING
William and Jane Jones
TO A GARDEN PARTY TO BE HELD AT
THEIR ADDRESS ON 21 JUNE FROM
2PM ONWARDS
DRESS INFORMAL
(BUT NO JEANS, T-SHIRTS, DEFINITELY NO
TRAINERS AND IF ANYONE TURNS UP
IN SHORTS THEY WON'T GET ACROSS
THE DOORSTEP)
RSVP

BILL: They're *your* friends. Tell me
what to wear.

JANE: Well, they'll be fairly **informal**.

BILL: So just my normal clothes?

JANE: No, I said informal, not **scruffy**.

BILL: I am not scruffy. **Casual**,
maybe. And I'm not going to
try to look **trendy** to please
your posh friends …

JANE: Nobody's saying that. I just
want you to look **smart** for
once.

BILL: I'll be **over-dressed**. I'll feel
stupid.

JANE: If you look OK, nobody will
know.

informal

scruffy

casual

trendy

smart

over-
dressed

Life at the top

My boyfriend thinks I'm really untidy.

Most nights, I get home from work quite late, and I'm really, really tired. If my shoes have laces, I never bother to **untie** them. I always think it's easier to do that before you **put** them **on**. So I just kick them off. Then I **unzip** my skirt. Usually I don't really **take** it **off** – I just let it fall to the floor. I **undo** the buttons on my blouse and **slip** it **off** – and sometimes it ends up on the floor too. After that I put on a T-shirt and a pair of loose trousers and pour myself a drink. My boyfriend thinks I'm really untidy – I wonder why?

untie

put on

unzip

take off

undo

slip off

Review 2

A Choose one word for each pattern.

plain checked spotted striped

1 with vertical lines from top to bottom
2 with small squares
3 with lots of dots
4 with no pattern, all one colour

B Match 1–3 with its opposite, a–c.

1 tight   a) short
2 long   b) loose
3 scruffy   c) smart

C Complete these with the correct material.

1 .... is light, strong and synthetic.
2 .... is warm and comes from sheep.
3 .... comes from a plant.

Shops

3

Where to shop

Take me to the Superstore!

GEORGE: The problem with life today is that nobody goes to the **high street shops** any more.

MARIA: What do you mean?

GEORGE: Well, we all just drive to out-of-town **shopping centres**, and go to **supermarkets** or **superstores**.

MARIA: Well, you can get things much cheaper there than at the **corner shop** or a town centre **department store**.

high street shop

shopping centre

supermarket

superstore

corner shop

department store

Quality

And this is the very latest slimming device to appear on the market. It may look a little **old-fashioned** at first glance, but it's a **high-quality** item, scientifically designed for maximum comfort and safety. It's **well-made**, from the finest materials, and it's a **stylish** addition to any home. It's also extremely **reliable** – it'll go on working for years if you take care of it. Now, let me show you just how easy it is to use …

old-fashioned

high-quality

well-made

stylish

reliable

Bargain store

JIM: Right, we need lots of bargains tomorrow. Put '**reduced** – £15 each' on all these sweaters.

BERT: That's still a bit **pricey**, isn't it? They normally sell at £16.

JIM: OK, let's make them a **special offer** – £30 for two. And a 5% **discount** to anyone who buys more than ten.

BERT: But boss, who's going to buy more than ten sweaters?

JIM: The same sort of idiot who believes we're having our third **closing-down sale** in six months!

reduce

pricey

special offer

discount

closing-down sale

How to pay

*And of course we accept all major **credit cards**.*

ASSISTANT: How are you paying?

CAROL: Sorry, I don't have **cash** with me.

ASSISTANT: We accept all major **credit cards**.

CAROL: I've come without my purse, and my cards are in it. Will you take a **cheque**?

ASSISTANT: Do you have a **bank card**?

CAROL: Sorry, that's in my purse, too. I wonder … could we arrange a **loan**?

ASSISTANT: For a pair of tights?

cash

credit card

cheque

bank card

loan

Complaining

I'd like to return this because I can't think of a use for it.

ALAN: I don't like to **complain**, but I bought this camera last week and it's stopped working.

ASSISTANT: Mmm – yes, it's **faulty**. Do you have your **receipt**? We can either **exchange** the camera or offer you a **credit note**. You can use it for anything in the shop.

ALAN: No, I'd rather have a **refund**.

ASSISTANT: I'm afraid that isn't company policy, sir.

ALAN: But it is the law – and I'm a law student. So refund my money or I'll see you in court. OK?

complain

faulty

receipt

exchange

credit note

refund

Review 3

A Match each description with a shop.

corner shop   department store
high street shop   supermarket

1 shop on the town's main street
2 small shop on any street in town
3 large shop that mainly sells food
4 large shop that sells almost everything

B Match these words with the descriptions.

cash   loan   discount   faulty   refund   reliable

1 a reduction in the usual price
2 your money returned to you
3 works well for a long time
4 money that you borrow
5 not working well
6 coins and banknotes

Travel
and
transport

The airport

We can't find the package anywhere.

I stood in the queue right behind him at the **check-in desk**. He was carrying a small package and I watched him check in two suitcases and get his **boarding pass**. Then I followed him through **passport control** and into the **departure lounge**. I had a seat beside him on the plane – I'd asked for that – and when we arrived I followed him to the **baggage hall** then here to **customs**. His suitcases are here but we can't find the package anywhere.

check-in desk

boarding pass

passport control

departure lounge

baggage hall

customs

Railway station

A: How much is a **return** to Stockford, coming back next Friday?

B: £118. A **single**'s half that price – £59.

A: Is that the **first-class** price?

B: No, that's a **standard** ticket. Do you want first class?

A: Er … no, standard's fine. What time's the next train?

B: In about two hours – at 4.15.

A: Is it **direct**?

B: No, you'll have to **change** at Allchurch.

return

single

first-class

standard

direct

change

Holiday hotel

single
room

double
room

suite

en suite

minibar

air
conditioning

Sunlife Hotel

76 single rooms

50 double rooms

3 suites

All with en suite
bathroom, minibar,
direct dial telephone,
satellite TV and
air conditioning.

DEPTH
1 METRE
NO DIVING

Fun in the sun

I know you're going to have a fantastic time here.

Hi! I'm Lee, your SunFun Tours rep – and this week we're really going to have fun in the sun! This evening there's a coach **excursion** to the beach for a **barbecue**. Tomorrow morning you'll enjoy **sunbathing** by the pool, then in the afternoon we have a short **cruise** around the islands, finishing with a **picnic** at the local Roman ruins. On Wednesday morning your coach will take you into town for some **sightseeing** and shopping, then in the evening a local folk-dancing group will entertain you …

excursion

barbecue

sunbathing

cruise

picnic

sightseeing

Getting home

delay

strike

strand

bomb scare

divert

But the flight home was awful … first of all we were **delayed** because of a **strike** somewhere and we were **stranded** at the airport. Then there was a **bomb scare**, so we had to go outside in the rain … and then, hours later, we finally took off, but when we arrived the plane couldn't land because of fog, so we were **diverted** to another airport. The whole journey was a nightmare!

Review 4

A Complete 1–8 with a–h.

1 Cruise: A holiday ....
2 Excursion: A short journey ....
3 Delayed: The plane left later ....
4 Customs: They sometimes open ....
5 Diverted: The plane is sent to a ....
6 Strike: Workers stop work for ....
7 Stranded: At the airport but you can't ....
8 Barbecue: A meal cooked outside on ....

a) an open fire.
b) for pleasure.
c) more money.
d) travel or leave.
e) on a ship.
f) different airport.
g) your suitcases.
h) than expected.

Friends
and
family

5

Names

*Do you remember that teacher at school – his **nickname** was The Frog?*

MAN: Hello. I'd like to check something in my account.

BANK: What's your account number, please? And your **surname**?

MAN: It's 1136538 and my family name's Jones.

BANK: And your **first name**, Mr Jones?

MAN: John. Well, that's my **middle name**. I hate my first name.

BANK: Yes, I have it on the screen – Hector. Now, I need your mother's **maiden name**.

MAN: It's James – before she married she was Cheryl James. But everybody used her **nickname** – Charlie. My dad thought she was a man at first.

surname

first name

middle name

maiden name

nickname

Relations

This is my half-brother.

KEN: You know, I've got two **brothers-in-law**. One of them, my wife's youngest brother, is still at primary school. But the other one, my sister's husband, has just retired.

IAN: Really? My father's just married again, and my **step-mother** already had two kids, so now I have a **step-brother** and a **step-sister**.

SUE: Is that so? My mum remarried too, and then had another baby, so I've got a **half-sister**.

brother-in-law

step-mother

step-brother

step-sister

half-sister

Mates

ROSE: So Tim's a **colleague** of yours?

STUART: Well, a **workmate** – we don't have 'colleagues' in the garage.

ROSE: Who's that he's talking to?

STUART: That's Liam. We were **room-mates** on holiday last year.

ROSE: Who's the other guy?

STUART: Joe? Oh, he used to be a **flatmate** – and we were **classmates** at school.

BOB: So … they're all your 'mates'?

STUART: No – I can't stand any of them.

colleague

workmate

room-mate

flatmate

classmate

This is my
flatmate.

Relationships

GAIL: Oh, hi Mum and Dad. This is Steve, my … **partner**.

DAD: Partner? You mean you work together?

GAIL: No, I mean … he's …

MUM: I think she means **boyfriend**. How nice!

GAIL: Well, a bit more than boyfriend …

DAD: Your **fiancé**? You're engaged?

GAIL: No, we live together.

DAD: So soon? I saw your **ex-husband** only last week. He was with his new **wife-to-be**. Such a nice guy, Clive.

partner

boyfriend

fiancé/ fiancée

ex-husband

wife-to-be

Feelings

can't
stand

fancy

fall out
with

make up

I **can't stand** my sister.
She makes me so mad.
She spies on my boyfriends,
And then she tells Dad.

I **fancy** *her* boyfriend,
But he **fell out with** me,
The day I told Dad
That she came in at three.

We might **make** it **up**
And then he might see
That he shouldn't have chosen
My sister ... but me!

*She spies
on my
boyfriends.*

Review 5

A Use these words in the sentences.

ex-husband   maiden   half-brother   nickname

1 She kept her .... name after marriage.

2 His .... is Lofty – because he's so tall.

3 He's my .... – same dad, different mums.

4 He's her .... now – they got divorced.

B Which relation are these people to me? Match 1–10 with a–d.

1 My wife's sister

2 My husband's mother

3 My wife's father

4 My husband's brother

5 My brother's wife

6 My husband's father

7 My wife's mother

8 My sister's husband

9 My wife's brother

10 My husband's sister

a) sister-in-law

b) brother-in-law

c) mother-in-law

d) father-in-law

Sport

6

Win, lose or draw

*Last time we played them we **lost** narrowly by six goals but this time we absolutely destroyed them by one goal to nil.*

And you join us at a tense moment in this game. Rangers were **leading** Rovers by one goal to nil. But young Sanchez has just **equalised** and … oh, he's **scored** again! That went straight through Bill Smith's legs and Rovers are ahead! Last Saturday they **lost** to City, but then **drew** with United in midweek. Today they might just **win**, especially with Bill Smith in goal. It really is time that man retired!

lead

equalise

score

lose

draw

win

The place to go

Right, lads, we'll swim this way.

JUAN: Jill, where's the football **stadium**?

JILL: There's no stadium here. The local **ground** is up that road, past the **tennis courts** and the **ice rink**. Why?

JUAN: I'm meeting my girlfriend there. Her father owns the club.

JILL: Stan Magee? You won't see him today. He'll be at the **golf course**.

JUAN: We're not going to the game anyway. We're off to the **swimming pool**.

stadium

ground

tennis court

ice rink

golf course

swimming pool

Hitting it

WORLD POOL CHAMPIONSHIP

Is this the pool queue?

SPEEDY SPORTS

SALE

GOLF CLUBS HALF PRICE

POOL CUES — AMAZING BARGAINS

CHEAPEST TENNIS RACKETS IN TOWN

TABLE TENNIS BATS 20% OFF

ICE HOCKEY STICKS REDUCED!!!

golf club

pool cue

tennis
racket

table
tennis
bat

ice
hockey
stick

Sporting types

*Even if the **referee** is your father, miss, you simply can't go around hitting anybody who calls him names.*

… and another advantage of being a **referee** is that it keeps me fit. You run a long way during a game – unlike, say, a tennis **umpire**, who spends all the time sitting down. Even if I'm working as an **assistant referee** – what we used to call a linesman – I run up and down the touchline for an hour and a half. And, of course, I get to meet all the famous players, as well as the **managers** and **coaches**.

referee

umpire

assistant referee

manager

coach

Dad and the lads

Now **catch** the ball, Tommy – there – oh, don't drop it! Now **kick** it back to daddy. No, kick it, don't **throw** it! Now, I'll kick it to you … now you **pass** it to Sammy. OK, Sammy, kick it back to me – really **hit** it hard. OK, now, we're going to practise something else – I'll throw it and you **head** it back. Don't be silly, of course it doesn't hurt! Ready?

catch

kick

throw

pass

hit

head

Review 6

A Put these words into pairs.

football   course   ice   court   swimming
pitch   tennis   pool   golf   rink

B Fill in the missing words.

*went ahead   equalised   win   lost   head
ground   passed*

A tense game at the City (1) .... today. The
visitors, United, (2) .... in the 11th minute when
Andic (3) .... to Minck and he scored. City (4) ....
ten minutes later when Kiselyov jumped up to
(5) .... a high ball into the net. It looked like
United might (6) .... when they got a penalty in
the final minute, but Miller missed. Then
Anson of City scored in injury time, so United
(7) .... for the third week in a row.

Health
and
medicine

7

Feeling bad

*Perhaps it's a **virus**. I've heard there's one going around …*

TESS: Oh, hi Bert – how are you?

BERT: Not too good. I've got a bad **cough** and a **sore throat**.

TESS: Your voice sounds a bit strange. Have you got a **temperature**?

BERT: I don't think so – well, maybe I feel a little hot.

TESS: It might be **flu**.

BERT: Yeah, possibly. But I won't bother the doctor. He'll just tell me to take an aspirin and go to bed.

TESS: Yes, you're probably right. Perhaps it's a **virus**. I've heard there's one going round.

cough

sore throat

temperature

flu

virus

Aches and pains

The pills that cure everything.

ALF: I keep getting these **headaches**.

DOCTOR: I see. When did they start?

ALF: Over a week ago. And I've got **earache** too, in my left ear.

DOCTOR: Well, I'll have a look at it.

ALF: I've got a **pain** in my right leg as well – did I tell you about that?

DOCTOR: No, Mr Gibb, you didn't.

ALF: And my **stomach ache** is so bad. I don't think I can go in to work this week. Worst of all, I've got **toothache**.

DOCTOR: Well, you'll have to see the dentist about that.

headache

earache

pain

stomach ache

toothache

At the doctor's

LUCY: So what did the doctor do?

EVAN: Well, she **examined** me. She put a thermometer in my mouth and took my temperature. She said it was normal.

LUCY: Did she listen to your **chest**?

EVAN: Oh yes. She said I should stop smoking, but apart from that, it was OK. Then she took my **blood pressure**.

LUCY: Fine too? Good. Anything else?

EVAN: Well, I asked if she wanted to take a **blood sample** but she said it wasn't necessary. It seems I'm perfectly healthy.

examine

chest

blood pressure

blood sample

Diagnosis

Hello, Emergency? I'd like you to send an ambulance to …

x

NURSE: I've seen the X-rays, and the Swiss doctor was right – your ankle isn't **broken**.

EMMA: Really? But it hurts a lot.

NURSE: Yes, it's badly **sprained**. Now, how's your shoulder – the one you **dislocated**?

EMMA: It's getting better – it's still a bit sore, though. But the **pulled** muscle in my leg has improved.

NURSE: And you **twisted** your knee?

EMMA: Yes, but that's OK now.

NURSE: I wonder – have you thought about giving up skiing?

broken

sprained

dislocated

pulled

twisted

Treatment

It was a table tennis accident. He won the game, jumped the net and fell off the table.

Mr Bonard, is it? Well, your arm is broken, but it's only a small crack, so there's no need to put it into **plaster**. I'm just going to give you an **injection** to take the pain away – there you are. Now we'll wait a few minutes and then I'll **bandage** it. No, of course you won't need an **operation**. I'll give you a **prescription**. Take it to the chemist's and get some painkillers in case you have trouble sleeping. That's all – and try not to use your arm for about six weeks.

plaster
injection
bandage
operation
prescription

Review 7

A Which of these can be followed by *ache*?

arm ear eye head knee leg stomach
tooth

B Make pairs with 1–10 and a–j.

1	flu	a) thermometer
2	cloth	b) injection
3	listen	c) shoulder
4	sore	d) bandage
5	pulled	e) chemist
6	needle	f) muscle
7	blood	g) pressure
8	dislocated	h) chest
9	prescription	i) virus
10	temperature	j) throat

Weather

8

Hot or cold?

What's that big yellow thing in the sky?

SUE: Brr! It's really **freezing** outside.

SAM: Yes, it is a bit **chilly**.

SUE: Chilly? It's so cold my nose almost dropped off. I don't understand you, Sam. Remember when we were in Spain, it was **boiling hot**, and you said it was quite **mild** really.

SAM: Yes, I suppose it was fairly warm.

SUE: Fairly warm? It was **scorching**! The temperature was above fifty!

freezing

chilly

boiling hot

mild

scorching

Wet or dry

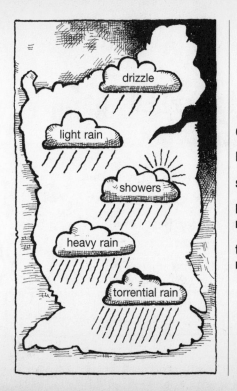

drizzle

light rain

shower

heavy rain

torrential rain

Windy weather

WIND SPEED GUIDE

THE YACHT CLUB

kph

1–6	Too calm. Stay in bar.
6–30	OK. Sail if you must.
30–50	Tricky. Best return to bar.
50–70	Do not leave bar!
70+	HIDE UNDER TABLE!

And now the weather forecast for weekend sailors. Saturday will begin with **breezes** in most areas. Later in the morning it will become more windy, with **light winds** in the south and some **high winds** further north. Make sure you're back on land by the evening, because there's a chance of **gales**, especially in the islands. Now, we're expecting a **hurricane** on Sunday morning, so, if possible, get your boat out of the water. Then go home and hide in the cellar for at least 24 hours. Sorry about that.

breeze

light wind

high wind

hurricane

gale

Visibility

So it looks like winter this year is going to be on Wednesday.

JAKE: Hello – 228 1665 – Jake here.

CARA: Jake, hi! It's me. How are you?

JAKE: Well, I'm missing you, and the weather's bad. It's been **foggy** all day.

CARA: Really? It's quite **bright** here.

JAKE: Well, it would be in Spain. It's been **dull** for ages here – the sky is **overcast** all the time. Everything's grey.

CARA: Well, we had some rain yesterday – but it was fairly **sunny** most of the time. Anyway, I didn't phone you to talk about the weather …

foggy

bright

dull

overcast

sunny

Snow and stuff

We expect to sell a lot of these when global warming really gets going.

And now the weather report for skiers. Some snow fell on the lower slopes this morning, but as the day warmed up this changed into **sleet**. In some southern resorts it actually rained, turning the snow on the ground into **slush**. But then the temperature dropped suddenly and the rain became **hail**. On the upper slopes the wind is rising quickly and any snow falls might become **blizzards**. Already, the wind is piling the snow up there into large **snowdrifts**. All in all, it isn't really a good day for skiing.

sleet

slush

hail

blizzard

snowdrift

Review 8

A Find pairs of words or phrases that have a similar meaning.

boiling hot   chilly   drizzle   dull   freezing
gale   hurricane   light rain   overcast
scorching

B Match these words with the definitions below.

*blizzard   sleet   breeze   snowdrift   slush
hail*

1 frozen rain
2 freezing rain
3 big snowstorm
4 very light wind
5 pile of snow made by wind
6 very wet snow on the ground

Work

9

A new job

So what did you do at university?

HELEN: Hey, I've been **offered** a job.

NIGEL: I didn't know you'd **applied** for one.

HELEN: Yes. I had an interview last week and they want me.

NIGEL: Are you going to **accept** it?

HELEN: Well, it's sixty miles away. I'd have to move.

NIGEL: Don't **turn** it **down** because of me. We can still see each other at weekends.

HELEN: Yes, and they said that if I get **promoted** I can move back here.

offer

apply

accept

turn down

promote

Making a living

*I play a
bit of
football.*

JESS: So what do you do?

SEAN: Oh, I play a bit of football.

JESS: No, I mean what do you **do for a living**? What's your job?

SEAN: Well, that's what I meant, really – I play football … for United. That's how I **make a living**.

JESS: Really? I'm in sport too. My company **deals with** sports publicity.

SEAN: Are you the people **in charge of** publicity for United?

JESS: Oh, sorry, I don't know. I only work there – I don't **run** the company.

do for a living

make a living

deal with

in charge of

run

Company man

So where are you going for your holiday this year?

There won't be any place for **unskilled** workers soon. Everything will be done by computers and robots. Even **skilled** workers will be rare. So if you want to get a job you'd better get some qualifications. Then you can be a **white-collar** worker, and if you work hard you could become a **manager**. You might even end up as a **company director**.

unskilled

skilled

white-collar

manager

company director

Nine to five

<table>
<tr><td>

nine-to-five

part-time

full-time

shift

flexi-time

job share

</td><td>

Actually, I've never had a **nine-to-five** job. I've done most things – I've worked **part-time**, sometimes two jobs at once. And I've done **full-time**, but that was working **shifts**, mainly at night. In my last job I was on **flexi-time** – I could start or finish when I wanted, within limits. Now I've got a **job share** arranged with one of my friends. Of course, I do other things as well …

</td></tr>
</table>

Your boss says **flexi-time** means flexible <u>hours</u>, not flexible days.

All gone away

maternity
leave

early
retirement

sick leave

make
redundant

sack

resign

STAFF AVAILABILITY

Mrs Brown: *On **maternity leave** till June.*

Mr Lin: ***Early retirement** starts today.*

Mr Smith: *On **sick leave** till next week.*

Ms Green: ***Made redundant** yesterday.*

Mrs Khan: *Called in sick.*

Mr Jones: ***Sacked** on Monday.*

Ms Black: *Too much to do – **resigned**!*

In the 21st century the **retirement** age will get lower and lower.

Review 9

Write a word or words in each space.

early retirement   maternity leave   promoted
sacked   turn down   runs   sick leave
part-time   shift   applied

1 Arthur's very ill. He's on .... now.
2 Joe was .... – he insulted the boss.
3 I've .... for a new job in Canada.
4 Who .... the shop when he's away?
5 I start at 11 pm, on the night-....
6 Don't .... that job. It's a good one.
7 He only works mornings – he's ....
8 Alan was .... to manager last week.
9 She's having a baby. She's on ....
10 He took .... and left work at 50.

Global
village

10

On TV

Actually, we don't have a TV. We feel they interfere with the children's education.

PAUL: How many TV channels do you get in your country?

LISA: Oh, quite a few – five **terrestrial** channels and lots of **satellite** ones.

PAUL: Are they any good?

LISA: Well, two of them are **public** channels – you pay a licence fee. The rest are **commercial** channels – but they have too many soaps and game shows.

PAUL: Do you get **cable** TV?

LISA: No, not in my part of town.

terrestrial

satellite

public

commercial

cable

On the phone

PAM: Hello. Can I help you?

SUE: Could you **put** me **through** to David Rix in Finance, please?

PAM: I'll **try** his **number**. Ringing for you now … no, there's no reply. Would you like to **hold the line**?

SUE: No. Could I **leave a message**? Ask him to **call** me **back** on my mobile. I'm going out.

PAM: That's fine … if you could just tell me your name, please?

put through

try a number

hold the line

leave a message

call back

Sunday papers

*I always find you get much better coverage with the **quality** papers.*

KEN: Have you finished with the paper?

ANN: Wait – I'm reading the **editorial**.

KEN: Hurry up! I'm stuck here with a **tabloid**. It's full of gossip. I want to look at a **quality** newspaper.

ANN: Read the Sunday **magazine**. It's on the table.

KEN: I don't want lifestyle **features**. I want to know what's going on. I'll read the **sports section** until you've finished.

editorial

tabloid

quality

magazine

features

sports section

Films

Subtitles are a problem in a country with three official languages.

PAULA: It's a great film. It's **set** in Russia at the time of the Revolution …

JUDY: It's a Russian film, then?

PAULA: No – it's French, actually, but it's been **dubbed** into English.

JUDY: So I'll have to read off the screen?

PAULA: No, dubbed, I said – not **subtitled**. There are some beautiful scenes. It was **shot** in St Petersburg.

JUDY: So when is it being **shown**?

set

dub

subtitle

shoot

show

Technology

digital camera

e-mail address

cybercafe

online

download

ALAN: OK, smile everybody! Thanks.

KARL: Can I have a copy of the photo?

ALAN: Well, it's a **digital camera**. Do you have an **e-mail address**?

KARL: Yes.

ALAN: OK, I'll e-mail it to you.

KARL: Great. I'll go to a **cybercafe**, get **online** and **download** it.

*So this is a **cybercafe!***

Review 10

A Make pairs with 1–5 and a–e.

1 PC   a) terrestrial
2 dubbed   b) tabloid
3 quality   c) commercial
4 public   d) subtitled
5 satellite   e) cybercafe

B Complete these sentences.

leave hold put call download shot set

1 He's in? OK, ... me through to him.
2 Can you .... the line for a minute?
3 Do you want to .... a message?
4 Ask her to .... me back, please.
5 I need to .... a file from the internet.
6 The film was .... in Texas in 1870 but it was
   actually .... in Spain.

Index

Your language

accept *v* /əksept/
Will you accept the job?
_____

air conditioning *n* /eə kəndıʃənıŋ/
Can you turn up the air conditioning?
_____

apply *v* /əplaɪ/
I applied for two jobs last week.
_____

assistant referee *n* /əsɪstənt refəri:/
An assistant referee saw the foul.
_____

baggage hall *n* /bægɪdʒ hɔ:l/
Your suitcases are in the baggage hall.
_____

baggy *adj* /bægi/
I don't like baggy trousers.
_____

bake *v* /beɪk/
Bake it in the oven for 35 minutes.
_____

bandage *n* /bændɪdʒ/
You need a bandage on that cut.
_____

bank card *n* /bæŋk kɑːd/
I've lost my bank card.
_____

bar *n* /bɑː/
Two bars of chocolate, please.
_____

Your language

barbecue n /ˈbɑːbɪkjuː/
There's a barbecue on the beach. _____

beat v /biːt/
Beat the egg whites for two minutes. _____

bland adj /blænd/
This is too bland – add more chilli. _____

blizzard n /ˈblɪzəd/
We get blizzards here in the winter. _____

blood pressure n /blʌd ˈpreʃə/
The nurse took my blood pressure. _____

blood sample n /blʌd ˈsæmpəl/
The doctor took a blood sample. _____

boarding pass n /ˈbɔːdɪŋ pæs/
Get your boarding pass at desk B. _____

boiling hot adj /ˈbɔɪlɪŋ hɒt/
It's boiling hot – everyone's swimming. _____

bomb scare n /bɒm skeə/
We left because of a bomb scare. _____

boyfriend n /ˈbɔɪfrend/
She's marrying her boyfriend. _____

Your language

catch *v* /kætʃ/
Catch the ball and throw it back. _____

change *v* /tʃeɪndʒ/
Do I have to change trains on the way? _____

checked *adj* /tʃekt/
He wore a red and white checked shirt. _____

check-in desk *n* /tʃek ɪn desk/
Take your luggage to the check-in desk. _____

cheque *n* /tʃek/
Can I pay by cheque? _____

chest *n* /tʃest/
Open your shirt. I'll listen to your chest. _____

chilly *adj* /tʃɪli/
Put a coat on – it's chilly outside. _____

classmate *n* /klæsmeɪt/
She was one of my classmates at school. _____

close-fitting *adj* /kləʊs fɪtɪŋ/
He looks good in close-fitting clothes. _____

closing-down sale *n* /kləʊzɪŋ daʊn seɪl/
There's a closing-down sale at the shop. _____

Your language

coach *n* /kəʊtʃ/
This team badly needs a new coach. _____

colleague *n* /kɒliːg/
We're colleagues but we're not friends. _____

commercial *adj* /kəmɜːʃəl/
The commercial channels show adverts. _____

company director *n* /kʌmpəni daɪrektə/
Her father's a company director. _____

complain *v* /kəmpleɪn/
I want to complain about the food. _____

corduroy *n* /kɔːdərɔɪ/
I don't like corduroy – it feels too rough. _____

corner shop *n* /kɔːnə ʃɒp/
I'll get some milk from the corner shop. _____

cotton *n* /kɒtn/
Cotton shirts need so much ironing. _____

cough *n* /kɒf/
I've got a bad cough. _____

credit card *n* /kredɪt kɑːd/
Can I pay by credit card? _____

Your language

credit note *n* /ˈkredɪt nəut/
Use this credit note in any of our shops. _____

cruise *n* /kruːz/
They went on a cruise in the Pacific. _____

customs *n* /ˈkʌstəms/
Customs searched my bags. _____

cybercafe *n* /ˈsaɪbə kæʃeɪ/
I'll download it at a cybercafe. _____

deal with *v* /diːl wɪð/
The police deal with terrible problems. _____

delay *v* /dɪleɪ/
The plane was delayed by bad weather. _____

department store *n* /dɪpɑːtmənt stɔː/
That department store sells everything. _____

departure lounge *n* /dɪpɑːtʃə laundʒ/
We waited in the departure lounge. _____

dessert *n* /dɪzɜːt/
We'll have fruit for dessert. _____

digital camera *n* /dɪdʒɪtəl kæmərə/
There's no film in a digital camera. _____

Your language

dinner *n* /dɪnə/
Do you have dinner at six or later? _____

direct *adj* /daɪrekt/
Is this train direct? _____

discount *n* /dɪskaʊnt/
This is cheap – there's a 20% discount. _____

disgusting *adj* /dɪsgʌstɪŋ/
The soup was disgusting. I sent it back. _____

dislocate *v* /dɪsləkeɪt/
He dislocated his shoulder in the gym. _____

divert *v* /daɪvɜːt/
We were diverted to this airport. _____

do for a living *v* /duː fər ə lɪvɪŋ/
I do it for a living but I hate the work. _____

double room *n* /dʌbəl ruːm/
We have 40 double rooms in this hotel. _____

download *v* /daʊnləʊd/
It takes ages to download pictures. _____

draw *n* /drɔː/
The result was a 1–1 draw. _____

Your language

drizzle *n* /ˈdrɪzəl/
I don't mind real rain but I hate drizzle. _____

dub *v* /dʌb/
The film was dubbed in French. _____

dull *adj* /dʌl/
The weather's dull and cloudy. _____

earache *n* /ˈɪəreɪk/
I'm not deaf – I've just got earache. _____

early retirement *n* /ˈɜːli rɪˈtaɪəmənt/
He took early retirement at 50. _____

editorial *n* /ˌedɪˈtɔːrɪəl/
This paper's editorial is about the war. _____

e-mail address *n* /ˈiːmeɪl ədres/
Give me your e-mail address. _____

en suite *adj* /ɒn swiːt/
Every room has an en suite bathroom. _____

equalise *v* /ˈiːkwəlaɪz/
It's 1–1. Rovers equalised a minute ago. _____

examine *v* /ɪɡˈzæmɪn/
The doctor examined my foot. _____

Your language

exchange *v* /ɪkstʃeɪndʒ/
Can you exchange this TV, please? _____

excursion *n* /ɪkskɜːʃən/
The beach excursion has been cancelled. _____

ex-husband *n* /eks hʌsbənd/
She remarried her ex-husband. _____

fall out with *v* /fɔːl aʊt wɪð/
Please don't fall out with her. _____

fancy *v* /fænsi/
He really fancies her older sister. _____

faulty *adj* /fɒlti/
This camera is faulty. _____

feature *n* /fiːtʃə/
I read a feature about drugs. _____

fiancé/fiancée *n* /fiɒnseɪ/
That's her fiancé – they're engaged. _____

first-class *adj* /fɜːst klæs/
There are no first-class seats. _____

first name *n* /fɜːst neɪm/
My first name's Arthur. _____

Your language

flatmate *n* /ˈflætmeɪt/
We were flatmates at college. _____

flexi-time *n* /ˈfleksitaɪm/
I'll get up later – I'm on flexi-time. _____

flu *n* /fluː/
Mr Barclay's not in today – he's got flu. _____

foggy *adj* /ˈfɒgi/
It isn't always foggy in London. _____

freezing *adj* /ˈfriːzɪŋ/
Let's go inside – it's freezing out here. _____

fry *v* /fraɪ/
Fry it in a little oil. _____

full-time *adj* /ˈfʊl taɪm/
She's a full-time writer. _____

gale *n* /geɪl/
You can't sail in a gale. _____

golf club *n* /ˈgɒlf klʌb/
He hit the burglar with a golf club. _____

golf course *n* /ˈgɒlf kɔːs/
He lives next to a golf course. _____

Your language

grate *v* /greɪt/
Grate the cheese and sprinkle it on top. _____

grill *v* /grɪl/
Grill the meat until it's brown. _____

ground *n* /graʊnd/
The football ground's around the corner. _____

hail *n* /heɪl/
The hail was bouncing off my umbrella. _____

half-sister *n* /hɑːf sɪstə/
My half-sister and I get on well. _____

head *v* /hed/
He headed the ball into the goal. _____

headache *n* /hedeɪk/
I've got a really bad headache. _____

heavy rain *n* /hevi reɪn/
We're expecting heavy rain so take care. _____

high street shop *n* /haɪ striːt ʃɒp/
Prices in high street shops are rising. _____

high wind *n* /haɪ wɪnd/
A high wind blew a tree down. _____

Your language

high-quality *adj* /haɪ kwɒlɪti/
This is a high-quality machine.　＿＿＿＿＿＿

hit *v* /hɪt/
Hit the ball harder!　＿＿＿＿＿＿

hold the line *v* /həʊld ðə laɪn/
He's engaged – please hold the line.　＿＿＿＿＿＿

hurricane *n* /hʌrɪkən/
There's a hurricane warning, so stay in.　＿＿＿＿＿＿

ice hockey stick *n* /aɪs hɒki stɪk/
He broke his ice hockey stick.　＿＿＿＿＿＿

ice rink *n* /aɪs rɪŋk/
They went skating at the ice rink.　＿＿＿＿＿＿

in charge of *prep* /ɪn tʃɑːdʒ əv/
She's in charge of the shop.　＿＿＿＿＿＿

informal *adj* /ɪnfɔːməl/
Wear informal clothes – no suit or tie.　＿＿＿＿＿＿

injection *n* /ɪndʒekʃən/
I need an injection before I go abroad.　＿＿＿＿＿＿

job share *n* /dʒɒb ʃeə/
Mary and Beth have a job share.　＿＿＿＿＿＿

Your language

kick *v* /kɪk/
Jones kicked the ball into the crowd. _____

lead *v* /liːd/
They were leading 2–1. _____

leave a message *v* /liːv ə mesɪdʒ/
Would you like to leave a message? _____

light rain *n* /laɪt reɪn/
It's just light rain – no need to worry. _____

light wind *n* /laɪt wɪnd/
It's a light wind but we can still sail. _____

loan *n* /ləʊn/
I got a loan to buy a new car. _____

loose *adj* /luːs/
I'd like a loose shirt for the beach. _____

lose *v* /luːz/
My team lost by two goals to one. _____

lunch *n* /lʌntʃ/
Can we have lunch at one-thirty? _____

magazine *n* /mægəziːn/
I like the photos in this magazine. _____

Your language

maiden name *n* /ˈmeɪdən neɪm/
Is Smith her maiden name?
_____

main course *n* /meɪn kɔːs/
We had steak for the main course.
_____

make a living *v* /meɪk ə ˈlɪvɪŋ/
You'll never make a living out of poetry. _____

make redundant *v* /meɪk rɪˈdʌndənt/
Fred was made redundant last week.
_____

make up *v* /meɪk ʌp/
Stop fighting, you two, and make it up. _____

manager *n* /ˈmænɪdʒə/
I'd like to speak to the manager, please.
_____

maternity leave *n* /məˈtɜːnɪti liːv/
She's on maternity leave.
_____

melt *v* /melt/
Melt the butter in a pan and add milk.
_____

middle name *n* /ˈmɪdl neɪm/
John's my middle name.
_____

mild *adj* /maɪld/
The weather is very mild.
_____

Your language

minibar *n* /mɪnɪbɑː/
There's no beer in the minibar. _____

nickname *n* /nɪkneɪm/
Her nickname's Ginger: it's the red hair. _____

nine-to-five /naɪn tə faɪv/
I've got a nine-to-five job. _____

nylon *n* /naɪlɒn/
Climbers use nylon ropes these days. _____

offer *v* /ɒfə/
He's happy – they've offered him a job. _____

old-fashioned *adj* /əʊld fæʃənd/
She has very old-fashioned ideas. _____

online *adv* /ɒnlaɪn/
His phone's engaged – he's online. _____

operation *n* /ɒpəreɪʃən/
She's a surgeon – she does operations. _____

overcast *adj* /əʊvəkɑːst/
The sky's overcast – it'll probably rain. _____

overcooked *adj* /əʊvəkʊkd/
The meat's so overcooked I can't eat it. _____

Your language

over-dressed *adj* /ˈəʊvədrest/
You'll look over-dressed with a tie. _____

packet *n* /ˈpækɪt/
Get me a packet of cornflakes, will you? _____

pain *n* /peɪn/
Lie down if you've got a pain. _____

part-time *adj* /pɑːt taɪm/
She worked part-time for a year. _____

partner *n* /ˈpɑːtnə/
Lucy's my partner – we're not married. _____

pass *v* /pɑːs/
Foster passed the ball back to Cook. _____

passport control *n* /ˈpɑːspɔːt kəntrəʊl/
They arrested him at passport control. _____

picnic *n* /ˈpɪknɪk/
The weather's wonderful for a picnic. _____

plain *adj* /pleɪn/
She wore a plain blue skirt. _____

plaster *n* /ˈplɑːstə/
Your arm's broken. You'll need plaster. _____

Your language

poach *v* /pəʊtʃ/
Poach the egg in hot water.　＿＿＿＿＿＿＿

pool cue *n* /puːl kjuː/
I can't play with a bent pool cue.　＿＿＿＿＿＿＿

prescription *n* /prəskrɪpʃən/
Take this prescription to the chemist's.　＿＿＿＿＿＿＿

pricey *adj* /praɪsi/
They're not cheap – they're very pricey.　＿＿＿＿＿＿＿

promote *v* /prəməʊt/
Charlie was promoted to manager.　＿＿＿＿＿＿＿

public *adj* /pʌblɪk/
Public TV channels are free.　＿＿＿＿＿＿＿

pull *v* /pʊl/
He has a pulled muscle.　＿＿＿＿＿＿＿

put on *v* /pʊt ɒn/
Wait – I'll just put on my shoes.　＿＿＿＿＿＿＿

put through *v* /pʊt θruː/
Mr Fry? I'll put you through to him.　＿＿＿＿＿＿＿

quality *adj* /kwɒlɪti/
It's a quality paper but it's very boring.　＿＿＿＿＿＿＿

Your language

receipt *n* /rɪˈsiːt/
Can you give me a receipt please? _____

reduce *v* /rɪˈdjuːs/
This shirt is reduced from £15 to £10. _____

referee *n* /refəˈriː/
The referee decided to send Bob off. _____

refund *n* /ˈriːfʌnd/
It doesn't work so I want a refund. _____

reliable *adj* /rɪˈlaɪəbəl/
My car isn't reliable – it's broken down. _____

resign *v* /rɪˈzaɪn/
I resigned from my job last week. _____

return *n* /rɪˈtɜːn/
A return to London please. _____

room-mate *n* /ˈruːm meɪt/
I had a room-mate at university. _____

run *v* /rʌn/
He ran a huge company for ten years. _____

sack *v* /sæk/
Joe was sacked for being late. _____

Your language

salty *adj* /sɒlti/
The Dead Sea is very salty.   _____

satellite *n* /sætəlaɪt/
Every house has satellite television.   _____

scorching *adj* /skɔːtʃɪŋ/
Let's go inside – it's scorching out here.   _____

score *v* /skɔː/
Lee scored two goals in two minutes.   _____

scruffy *adj* /skrʌfi/
You look so scruffy – tidy yourself up.   _____

set *v* /set/
The film was set in Russia.   _____

shift *n* /ʃɪft/
The workers do three shifts a day.   _____

shopping centre *n* /ʃɒpɪŋ sentə/
The shopping centre has 30 shops.   _____

short *adj* /ʃɔːt/
That skirt is too short for a funeral.   _____

shoot *v* /ʃuːt/
Tom Hanks' last film was shot in Italy.   _____

Your language

show *v* /ʃəʊ/
The film was shown twice last week. _____

shower *n* /ʃaʊə/
There are usually showers in April. _____

sick leave *n* /sɪk liːv/
He was on sick leave after the accident. _____

sightseeing *n* /saɪtsiːɪŋ/
I hate sightseeing – I'll be swimming. _____

simmer *v* /sɪmə/
Reduce the heat and simmer the soup. _____

single *adj* /sɪŋgəl/
Just a single – I'm not coming back. _____

single room *n* /sɪŋgəl ruːm/
Two people can't sleep in a single room. _____

skilled *adj* /skɪld/
You have to train to be a skilled worker. _____

sleet *n* /sliːt/
It's cold. The rain's turning into sleet. _____

slip off *v* /slɪp ɒf/
Let me slip off my jacket and sit down. _____

Your language

slush *n* /slʌʃ/
It's too warm – you can't ski on slush. _____

smart *adj* /smɑːt/
These soldiers don't look very smart. _____

snack *n* /snæk/
I'd like a snack – a sandwich perhaps? _____

snowdrift *n* /snəʊdrɪft/
There were snowdrifts beside the road. _____

sore throat *n* /sɔː θrəʊt/
He's not coming. He's got a sore throat. _____

sour *adj* /saʊə/
Put some more sugar in – this is sour. _____

special offer *n* /speʃəl ɒfə/
They're half price – it's a special offer. _____

spicy *adj* /spaɪsi/
I like Indian food because it's so spicy. _____

sports section *n* /spɔːts sekʃən/
I only want the sports section. _____

spotted *adj* /spɒtəd/
He wore a red and white spotted tie. _____

Your language

sprained *adj* /spreɪnd/
Your wrist is sprained – it isn't broken. _____

stadium *n* /steɪdiəm/
The Olympic stadium is magnificent. _____

standard *adj* /stændəd/
Is that a standard or a first-class ticket? _____

starter *n* /stɑːtə/
I'll have the soup as a starter. _____

steam *v* /stiːm/
If you steam fish it keeps its flavour. _____

step-brother *n* /step brʌðə/
My step-brother's surname is different. _____

step-mother *n* /step mʌðə/
I liked my new step-mother. _____

step-sister *n* /step sɪstə/
We're not related – she's my step-sister. _____

stir *v* /stɜː/
Stir the milk into the flour and butter. _____

stomach ache *n* /stʌmək eɪk/
Prawns always give me a stomach ache. _____

Your language

strand *v* /strænd/
We were stranded at Rome for hours. _____

strike *n* /straɪk/
The teachers are on strike again. _____

striped *adj* /straɪpt/
The prisoners wear striped uniforms. _____

stylish *adj* /staɪlɪʃ/
That new dress isn't stylish at all. _____

subtitle *v* /sʌbtaɪtəl/
This film was subtitled very badly. _____

suede *adj* /sweɪd/
Suede jackets don't look good on me. _____

suite *n* /swiːt/
The hotel has five luxury suites. _____

sunbathing *n* /sʌnbeɪðɪŋ/
Sunbathing can be dangerous. _____

sunny *adj* /sʌni/
I like gardening on sunny days. _____

supermarket *n* /suːpəmɑːkɪt/
Nobody speaks to you in supermarkets. _____

superstore *n* /ˈsʊpəstɔː/
We got our furniture in the superstore. _____

surname *n* /ˈsɜːneɪm/
Is Lee your surname or your first name? _____

swimming pool *n* /ˈswɪmɪŋ puːl/
The swimming pool is 25 metres long. _____

table tennis bat *n* /ˈteɪbəl tenɪs bæt/
Table tennis bats come in many colours. _____

tabloid *n* /ˈtæblɔɪd/
There's a lot of rubbish in the tabloids. _____

take off *v* /teɪk ɒf/
He's too tired to take off his clothes. _____

temperature *n* /ˈtempərətʃə/
Take Bob's temperature – he looks ill. _____

tennis court *n* /ˈtenɪs kɔːt/
There are very few grass tennis courts. _____

tennis racket *n* /ˈtenɪs rækət/
Wooden tennis rackets are out of date. _____

terrestrial *adj* /təˈrestriəl/
We have terrestrial TV channels. _____

Your language

throw *v* /θrəʊ/
He can throw a football 50 metres.
_____

tight *adj* /taɪt/
This skirt's tight – I've put on weight.
_____

tin *n* /tɪn/
We'd better get some tins of soup, too.
_____

toothache *n* /tuːθeɪk/
Toothache? Well, go to the dentist.
_____

torrential rain *n* /tərenʃəl reɪn/
There is often torrential rain here.
_____

trendy *adj* /trendi/
She's so trendy – always fashionable.
_____

try a number *v* /traɪ ə nʌmbə/
Could you try Mark's number, please?
_____

tube *n* /tjuːb/
We need a new tube of toothpaste.
_____

turn down *v* /tɜːn daʊn/
I turned down the job. I didn't want it.
_____

twist *v* /twɪst/
I twisted my knee when I fell.
_____

Your language

umpire *n* /ˈʌmpaɪə/
Tennis umpires sit in high chairs. _____

undo *v* /ʌnˈduː/
It's difficult to undo all these buttons. _____

unskilled *adj* /ʌnˈskɪld/
Unskilled workers have no training. _____

untie *v* /ʌnˈtaɪ/
I can't untie the knots on this parcel. _____

unzip *v* /ʌnˈzɪp/
Could you help me to unzip this dress? _____

virus *n* /ˈvaɪrəs/
You've got a virus. Go to bed. _____

well-made *adj* /wel ˈmeɪd/
It's quite cheap and not very well-made. _____

whisk *v* /wɪsk/
Whisk the sauce until it's smooth. _____

white-collar *adj* /waɪt ˈkɒlə/
He's a white-collar worker now. _____

wife-to-be *n* /waɪf tə ˈbiː/
His wife-to-be is very rich. _____

Your language

win *v* /wɪn/
I think the best team won. _____

wool *n* /wʊl/
We get wool and meat from sheep. _____

workmate *n* /wɜːkmeɪt/
I liked my workmates in the factory. _____

Answers

Review 1

A 1 lunch   2 snack   3 sour   4 bland   5 starter
  6 dessert

B 1b 2d 3e 4a 5c

Review 2

A 1 striped   2 checked   3 spotted   4 plain

B 1b 2a 3c

C 1 nylon   2 wool   3 cotton

Review 3

A 1 high street shop   2 corner shop   3 supermarket
  4 department store

B 1 discount   2 refund   3 reliable   4 loan   5 faulty
  6 cash

Review 4

1e 2b 3h 4g 5f 6c 7d 8a

Review 5

A 1 maiden   2 nickname   3 half-brother
  4 ex-husband

B 1a 2c 3d 4b 5a 6d 7c 8b 9b 10a

Review 6

A football pitch   ice rink   swimming pool   tennis court
golf course

B 1 ground   2 went ahead   3 passed   4 equalised
5 head   6 win   7 lost

Review 7

A ear, head, stomach, tooth

B 1i 2d 3h 4j 5f 6b 7g 8c 9e 10a

Review 8

A boiling hot/scorching; chilly/freezing; drizzle/light rain;
dull/overcast; gale/hurricane

B 1 hail   2 sleet   3 blizzard   4 breeze   5 snowdrift
6 slush

Review 9

1 sick leave   2 sacked   3 applied   4 runs   5 shift
6 turn down   7 part-time   8 promoted
9 maternity leave   10 early retirement

Review 10

A 1e 2d 3b 4c 5a

B 1 put   2 hold   3 leave   4 call   5 download
6 set/shot